A Book Of Thoughts:

Poems By Betty Maier

iUniverse, Inc.
New York   Bloomington

A Book Of Thoughts: Poems By Betty Maier

iUniverse books may be ordered through booksellers or by contacting:

iUniverse
1663 Liberty Drive
Bloomington, IN 47403
www.iuniverse.com
1-800-Authors (1-800-288-4677)

ISBN: 978-1-4401-5473-7 (pbk)
ISBN: 978-1-4401-5474-4 (ebk)

Printed in the United States of America

iUniverse rev. date: 7/29/2009

TABLE OF CONTENTS

DEDICATION vii
PREFACE...ix
COOKIES AND CANDY..1
RAIN 2
SNOW...3
THE ANSWER IS IN THE SKY 4
THE FAIR 5
HARVEY MOON 6
HALLOWEEN 7
MY SYMBOL...8
GIFT OF LIFE FOR THE TURKEY...9
THE WORD...10
CHRISTMAS MEMORIES...13
THE HOLEY BUCKET 14
TEEBIE, TEEBIE, WHERE ARE YOU TEEBIE.........................16
THE GREAT BEAR HUNT..17
A DOG..18
MR. SLIM 20
TRUST...22
THE BEAR WHO FORGETS TO HIBERNATE.........................23
IS IT SOUP YET? 24
ONLY THE SHADOW KNOWS..26
I DON'T WANT TO BE A COWBOY 27
WHAT HAPPENED? 28
I LOVE YOU MR. FEBUS..29
PLEASE DIM THE LIGHTS...30
I WANNA RIDE BULL 31
TAINTED WATERS...32
I'M NOT A LOSER...33
TO EACH HIS OWN...35
LIFE 37
A TRIBUTE TO MY FATHER...39
DEATH HAS NO FEELING FOR YOU OR ME.........................41
MAMMA..43

YOUR PRESENCE 44
POVERTY 45
THE CRY'S OF OUR CHILDREN 46
DISPLACED HOMEMAKER..48
SAMANTHA BILLIEDELIGHT..50
MICHAEL 51
STACY...52
IT'S NOT THE END 54
SABELLE..56
MY HUSBAND 58
CHARLES 60
IS IT TIME ? 61
FOR MY BROTHERS 62
AS TIME GOES BY 63
FOR THOSE WHO HAVE TOUCHED MY LIFE.......................64

DEDICATION

This book is dedicated to all the people who created my life experiences.

PREFACE

"A Book of Thoughts, Poems by Betty Maier" is literally just that, I poured my heart out in this book which allows me to empty my emotional tank. I have many things bottled up in this tank as I'm sure most of you do. We all need an outlet and this book is my outlet. I hope you can relate to my way of thinking or at least learn a different perspective on these issues. Enjoy and try to read this with an open mind. Who knows maybe I will sway you to my way of thinking. This has been an ultimate pleasure.

A BOOK OF THOUGHTS, POEMS BY BETTY MAIER

COOKIES AND CANDY

Chocolate Chip, peanut butter,
What are those words I'm hearing you mutter?
Snickerdoodle, sugar, and gingerbread,
Boy these calories I'm going to dread.

What is it you are talking about?
I bet you're getting ready to bake without a doubt.

I need ginger, nutmeg, and cinnamon,
I can't wait until they are all done.

Come on tell me please,
Are those cookie recipes I see?
The next thing she will be talking about is candy,
My taste buds are going to be doing just dandy.

This time of the year I love,
Who cares about clothes fitting tighter then a glove.

These are the things I will never forget,
Smell that? Are they done yet?

RAIN

Do you know what I do when it rains?
I run for my grandmother's kitchen and I let my sense of smell go
    insane.
This is when she begins to bake cinnamon rolls, cookies and cake.
Not eating these is more than I can take.

When you look into her oven,
You see the juice from the luscious apples bubbling.
Boy take a whiff of that apple pie if it doesn't hurry up I'll cry.

She makes this a special day and it's doesn't matter that we can't play.
We take out our arts and crafts while looking at the things we create
    makes us laugh.

The house is all warm and toasty and the crackling fire smells of apple
    wood roasting.
Here she comes with a cookie and a cup of hot chocolate one to eat
    and one for your pocket.

When that smell is in the air,
Into my grandmother's kitchen I'll tear.

SNOW

Winter's come and go but this does not guarantee that it will snow.
When we are older we hope that it won't this night,
When we are young and full of delight we just want to see the world
    beautiful and white.

When we are older the cold tells our bodies our time here is almost
    done.
I guess when you are young snow makes the world full of fun.

So while you are young, go play in the snow,
Through the window I will watch when I grow old.

THE ANSWER IS IN THE SKY

I looked at the heavens the other night and I seen a star falling like a
   streak of light.
I couldn't help but detect the presence of sorrow as I ask myself about
   tomorrow.
I wonder if the answer will ever be found?
Not if we never look any further than the ground.

It appears to me for every child that is born there is a new star to be
   adorn.
For every star that falls across the sky I know there is someone who
   has just died.

A star can stand for each one of us; after all, we are made of the same
   stuff.
There's a purpose for all life, you know, he puts us down here to grow.

There's no use to run when our time comes because he'll weed out the
   star that stands for you and me,
He lets it fall deep within the sea.

There's a connection between you and me with the stars we see.
The answer is right before our eyes; all we need to do is study the sky.

THE FAIR

Let's all go to the Central Washington State Fair!
There are lots of scary rides if you dare!
Hurry there's the booth where the tickets are sold!
Come one, come all, young and old.

The fair's a place to go I've been told where you will never feel old.
It's a fact that as long as you feel young your days' end will take longer
    to come.

So find your youth as you are challenged at the booths,
Win a prize as you enjoy being alive.
Eat until your heart's content,
A fair is a true God sent.

Capture this feeling and put it in a jar,
It isn't as silly as wishing on a star!
Let's go gather some more memories to share,
Let's all go to the Central Washington State Fair.

HARVEY MOON

Harvey Moon's returning to town,
It's ok to act like a clown.
He's the one with the pumpkin head and scarecrow clothes.
He's the one we wait for every year don't you know.

It's that time of the year everyone will fear.
The leaves are no longer green,
It's truly the season of Halloween.

The jingle you hear reassures us that he is near.
Excitement is displayed all around when we know Harvey Moon's
    returning to town.

Come one, come all!
Let's have a ball.
When there are pumpkins on the ground, Harvey Moon is back in
    town.

HALLOWEEN

Trick or treat, smell my feet,
Give me something good to eat,
This Halloween night is going to be neat.

Little do I know I will not get to go.
My little brother has a plan of his own, me spending this evening at
    home.

I am really innocent,
Into the orchard he hurriedly went.
Secretly adding tar to the mud and leaves; you see this is the way he
    will blame everything on me.
I just wanted to make our house scary, not all sticky, black and hairy.
This takes the paint right off the houses' side,
There is no where for me to hide.

Isn't there anything I can do?
The sheets for the costumes I ruined are only a few.
I will help you paint and clean please don't be so mean!
The house really doesn't look that bad,
Look at my little brother, he's glad.

Okay I'll spend the whole night at home sitting in this dark place all
    alone!
Don't let it bother you when our friends come by,
This guilt trip is not working at least I gave it a try.

Trick or treat, smell my feet,
Give me something good to eat.
This Halloween night I will only get the trick not the treat.

MY SYMBOL

I wish people were more like a butterfly,
If so maybe we can help our young live not die.
Their different colors can stand for the human race,
Each and everyone should be made to feel special in this place.
They spread their wings so wide and straight,
And you just know something that beautiful feels no hate.

They start out as something mighty ugly but even they can change
    and I must say quite smugly.
They don't have too long to live but while they are here they sure have
    a lot to give.

So you see when I look at a butterfly I pay no heed to this world full
    of lies.
All the different colors of the human race make me realize that all of
    us have an equal right to take our place.

The sincerity and peace about their fight tell me my feeling about
    them is right.
We to may start out wrong but we can always change ourselves and
    try to belong.
We to have a short time to be here so let's make sure our reason for
    being in this world will always be near.
Let's all take a closer look at the beautiful butterfly and help the
    young live not die.

GIFT OF LIFE FOR THE TURKEY

Does man always conquer his game?
Maybe unless it becomes tame.
If it cannot out run the man, there's other ways to take a stand.

A man has feelings the game does not.
This creates the beginning of the game's plot.

A lot is at stake this is all it takes,
He becomes a friend with the big one so his deed is almost done.
The end is here don't fear the man will not allow the little ones to
    shed a tear.

You can hear the game snicker and say,
I've won this battle and I will live another day.
Does man always conquer his game?
Maybe unless he thinks the game becomes tame.

THE WORD

Love is the most misused word in any language,
What a shame because if you set the stage,
The word has the power to change darkness to light,
Or take away someone's plight.

It can give life or take it away, it can make you want to go or stay.
And usually I'm sorry to say if yours has gone astray,
You'll feel the negative version now being played.

You start out as a child receiving parental love that is not mild.
There's a lot you will be able to endure because they make you feel so
    secure.
You know while you are sleeping there's no reason for any weeping.
All your childhood problems that are there,
Will be taken care of by mommy and daddy with no despair.

You have no worry of food and clothing,
Or whether Santa will fill your stocking.
No worries of big bad monsters entering your room,
As you know they will be there with one big yell really soon.

They are always there patting you on the head and wiping the tears
    away,
So you have a bond of love that even harsh words can't take it astray.
Most mothers' love for her child is one of protection and affection,
Teaching them to be of your reflection.
This love is grand and strong.

Raise your children the best you can,
With love, understanding, and patience that God shows man,
Put out your hand as parents do all across the land.
Allow them to be children and make mistakes but give them a break.
Think of yourself when you were young give them some credit and
    thy will be done.

You must know this love is different because you're raising your child
     to go on his own,
And start the cycle as he's been shown.
From baby's first cry a mother hears,
Makes the link started nine months prior impossible to tear.
Even with animal's motherhood is understood,
They fight for their cub until they die, I might add with a hell of a lot
     of pride.
This instinct is given to a mother from God,
This is the understanding we obtain from above.

The time will draw near when you will hear,
Sweetheart it's your turn now, you lead the world as I've shown you
     how.
The clock says right now.

At first you are afraid and a little dismayed.
What will I do now that I've been betrayed, children you are
Wrong, you are turned loose because you are now strong.
The past is gone and now it is time to begin the long line.
The line will take you far and wide if you travel wisely and with pride.
Don't forget the gift from above; share it sparingly this type of knowl-
     edge and love.

Now think back about the love for your sisters and brothers,
This is a lot different than the love from your mother.
You laughed and cried and watched each other grow, you know some-
     day they have to go.
Span out and start your lives with someone new,
You see they have to share with others too.
You will love them faults and all,
And you will be there if they fall.

You think you've meant the perfect one, the one that is chosen for
     you by the almighty son.
This love will be the most important one of all,

The others are good but if you recall, this is when
God gives you the right to go hand in hand walking tall.

The love of a husband and a wife should be for your whole life.
You share your minds, your body, your life,
And only tenderness should be your strife.
Caring about each other's feelings, touching softly is your whole
   being.

You see you are starting a new generation,
Thank God you have the chance to be in participation.

Walk softly my friend, as you will see, one harsh word can grow like a
   tree.
Once said and done is like burning the cross, nothing but ashes and
   then the dust.
It's such a shame to play these games before you know it you're look-
   ing at those gates with your name inflamed.

Cherish each other with all your souls,
It's mighty lonesome when you are old.
There is no love like the one between a husband and wife,
This should be your ultimate goal for your life.

CHRISTMAS MEMORIES

This is the time of the season you will hear,
I love this time of the year.
On my face you will see sorrow,
Never wanting this day to be tomorrow.

Close your eyes and you will see a past Christmas that is full of
   beautiful memories.
Smell the aroma of cookies, homemade candy, and fresh baked
   apple pie?
I have to have a piece or I'll just die!

There's the pine smell from the tree,
It grows just for you and me.
Do you see the whole family hanging bulbs and candy canes?
Oh what a beauty, will it always be the same?
It's time to lay the presents below,
Here's one with my name and here's one for you to claim.

Memories are what you want to give,
Each one will always be relived.
Remember as the years go by,
There will be others closing their eyes.

Create beautiful thoughts and dreams that will stay,
So that someone after you will be able to say that he to loves this day.

THE HOLEY BUCKET

I know a secret place where no one will recognize your face.
It's a world full of fantasies,
No one is allowed there but you and me.

We can be Tarzan or Jane,
It really doesn't matter what name,
We can be wild not tame.
There's no adult games don't you see,
In this place we can be free.

We can laugh or cry,
We can pretend to die.
We can become blood brothers,
Or swing from one tree to another.

We must be careful though,
There are signs of danger so I've been told.
We can't let this game get out of hand,
We're not quite old enough to take a stand.

Remember if something does go wrong,
We have to be very strong.
Where there's a will there's a way,
So most adults say!

We'll use the techniques that work at home,
After all it should be understood that we aren't totally grown.
A bucket may be the answer to this game,
But we must remember even in this place of dreams,
A bucket with holes is not the same so it seems.

This is a world of fantasies,
But there is still a world of reality.
As quick as a fire burns,
This world can turn,
Into a world of adults without a doubt,
They'll have to rescue you and me from this world of fantasies.

TEEBIE, TEEBIE, WHERE ARE YOU TEEBIE

Someday I'm sure you'll understand,
This kind of life for you wasn't planned.
You will soon grow out of this,
I know until then a lot you will miss.

Your mother loves you very much,
Dealing with your illness is very tough.
She doesn't want you to go away,
Won't you please stay?

There is a little boy that has many toys,
These are not as much fun as being able to go outside and run.

Why is she being so mean to me?
I just want her to let me be free.
I don't care if I do get sick, I think this is all a great big trick!

Why can't I be like the rest and play,
I don't believe anything you say!
Listen to her yell,
I'll sneak out this back door, don't tell.

I'm buying penny candy,
They'll play with me.
Things will be fine and dandy you'll see.

I'm going to find somewhere to play,
I'm going to run away!
I don't care if she does look for me,
All she ever says is Teebie, Teebie, Where are you Teebie!

THE GREAT BEAR HUNT

Get your bullets,
Get your gun.
We have a man's job to get done!

It doesn't matter what the prey,
Deer, elk, bear, pheasant, or grouse,
We will be proud to say,
There will always be meat in our house.

Davy Crockett, Daniel Boone,
The great bear hunt will determine which one fits this really soon.
Will it be Kent, John, Dave, Ron, or Ken?
You will not find out until the end.

Let's see who will tell the biggest story,
Let's see whom walks away with all the glory.
We will fix his egotistical ways,
This is what we're going to say.
Now what guys?
Can you believe John fell for this disguise?

Who's going to tell him?
Not you or I,
I'm a friend; He'll believe this until he dies or until the end.
We will never bring it up again.

A DOG

What does a dog really mean to you other than chewing your brand
    new shoe?
Is he your little boy's toy that is supposed to give him joy?
Is he a whim for the day?
Something that will be there for play!
If he's lucky you'll let him stay.

I think he's truly man's best friend,
If loved he'll stay with you until the end.

I believe he can talk,
Who's to say the dog may do it in his own way.
I've meant some humans who can only sit and squawk!

I know that he's always there,
I know that he really cares.
It doesn't matter if I'm healthy or sick,
He always shows me attention really quick.

I feel really bad,
When I look into a dog's eyes and realize he's sad.
When they are no longer young to some they are no longer any fun.

Let's leave them in the back yard and pretend that they are going to
    be our guard.
Which for me to believe is hard.

I think the newness has worn away,
It's time now to say hey, go away!
What does a dog really mean to you?
Is he a toy for your own amusement to use?

Wouldn't it be nice if he could put you on ice,
And give you a stinky shoe to chew!
Would you be as true blue as he is to you?
What does a dog really mean to you?

MR. SLIM

Hello Mr. Slim where have you been?
Out collecting more marbles and rocks, can I look in your socks?

I'll make you a special pouch to keep these in,
I like doing things for my best friends.
Look at all the pretty colors,
These are a lot prettier than my brothers.

Do you have any Pury's in there?
If you do can we share?
I have three Black Beauty's,
I'll trade one for a Pury.

This Ellensburg Blue rock is your best,
It's really different from the rest.
It is perfect for a ring,
You have so many beautiful things.

Have you found any more oil lamps?
They are perfect to have when you camp.
This one is new,
Wow what a pretty blue.
It even has a handle on it,
If mother sees this, she'll have a fit.

You say you have no family to give these pretty things to,
I promise you I'd clean and shine them the way you do!
You mean a lot to us,
It's not fare to have your specialty's lay around and collect dust.
Your marbles and rocks will bring beautiful memories so let me take-
     care of them when you are gone, please?

Here I made this pouch for you,
It reads, "from a person that you knew."
A family's love for you grew and your life will never end.
Thank you for these things my friend.

TRUST

Children are so innocent; they are definitely God sent.
The little faces are all a glow and they pick you up when you feel low.
They bring laughter and cheer into our lives without them
    we'd surely die.

They look at you with total trust,
Honesty is a must.
You need to be careful with what you say,
You may have to explain it someday.

You may see your little one,
Taking what you say for granted,
The seed is already planted.
The deed will have already been done.

I know it's cute and funny too but you wouldn't want this to happen
    to you.
A little kidding is okay as long as they know it's only play.

I wouldn't want to look into his eyes and try to explain the difference
    between a joke and a lie.
It will not only embarrass him but also you,
He may learn to only trust a few.

It's better to remember there is only one fact,
You are responsible for their every act.

Let's give our child a reason to trust,
For them to live a good life this is a must.
Again a little kidding is okay as long as they know it's only play.

THE BEAR WHO FORGETS TO HIBERNATE

Oh what webs we weave when we try to deceive.
Our minds become all twisted and in this no one assisted.

It seems so real this is a raw deal.
If it weren't for that silly old bear we wouldn't be in this mess,
The rest wouldn't care.

He wouldn't hibernate,
I guess we're the ones who took the bait.
Now what do we do?
If we only knew!
The trouble we are in no one will be our friend!

I'm not going to tell do you hear me I yell!
Please do not tease me we didn't mean to deceive!
I guess we have to face this; mom reaches over and gives me a kiss.
I walk out the door with my hands in a fist!

Heroes we have not become after it's all been said and done.
There has to be another way,
I know exactly what I'll say!

What a silly old bear,
It's too late,
It's him I hate.
He forgot to hibernate!

IS IT SOUP YET?

Shall I do this now or shall I do that?
I feel like a mad hatter,
Rat a tat tat!

How many days do I have left?
When will I have time to rest?
I shouldn't think about this right now but I need to get it done
    somehow!

I can't get sick,
I'll find help but whom do I pick?
I can't ask just anyone,
They'll make sure it doesn't get done.

They may want my position,
Boy this is a big decision.
I know there's mom,
To my aid she will come.
I really feel dumb.

What am I so worried about?
She'll take care of things without a doubt.
It feels as though I've burned up my brain,
I think I'm going insane!

I don't feel very well,
On these troubles I shouldn't have dwelled.
I've done it now,
It's time to throw in the towel!

I will go to bed and cover up my head; I might as well be dead!

What's that smell?
I can just about bet.
Why did I fret?
Okay soon I will be well.

Boy I had a bad dream,
It is so real so it seemed.
Those were deadlines I could never have met.
Hey mom is it soup yet?

ONLY THE SHADOW KNOWS

One of these days the biggest game ever we will play.
I'm tired of you taking my things.
I will have the last smile and you will hear me sing while remember-
    ing I'm the king!

You will never out fox me don't you see,
I'm the wittiest person there ever will be!
You might just as well take the back seat,
My idea can't be beat!

Tug and pull try to break the chain,
If you think this will work you are insane or a jerk!
Cry to mom all you want tears will do no good to flaunt!

I have a surprise waiting for you,
Only if you knew.
You will see me dance,
At your face I will do more than glance!

I will be all a glow when you read,
"Only the shadow knows!"

I DON'T WANT TO BE A COWBOY

So what if I tell a few lies, I only want to be one of the guys.
You have no right to treat me this way, just give in and let me play.
I think you've carried it a little too far, I'd be better off if you cover me
    in tar!
Remember who I am,
I'm more than just a friend.
Following you around and snitching are what sister's do,
I thought this was one thing that you knew.

Okay, my mother's number one son, I will never bother you again!
I concede this game you will win.
I won't even try to be your friend!

So what if I tell a few lies, I only wanted to be one of the guys.
You can be the Indian boy but I will never again be the cowboy!

WHAT HAPPENED?

What happened?
I want to be told.
I just wanted the new in and throw out the old,
I didn't mean to be so bold.

When did things get out of hand?
Was it when we felt that our words meant no more than a grain of
    sand,
Or was it because we wanted the right to choose or the right to win
    or lose,
Or how about the right to say I want to do this or that today?

Does it really matter how we dress?
This has nothing to do with our lives becoming a mess.
What does make-up really do?
I don't see how it changed you.

I only want to stand up and be counted, instead the tension has really
    mounted.
Maybe I was too young to try but when would it change, after we've
    died?
This has really been strange.

What happened, where are you and I?
I just wanted the new in and throw away the old.
What happened?
I still have not been told!

I LOVE YOU MR. FEBUS

Doesn't anything ever last?
Do we have to grow old so fast?
A true friend I've found in you and I will never bid you ado.

You hold me in your arms so tight, I know that this is the only thing
that is right.
Even though at times I am up and then I am down,
You never make me feel like a clown.

I don't know what's in store for me, maybe you can tell me my
destiny.
What happened my friend?
Do we have to say good-by?
Is this the end?

Am I getting too big for you to hold or is it what I've been told?
Doesn't anything ever last?
Do we have to grow old so fast?

This is not what I had planned, in my back yard you should always
stand.
This has been taken out of our hands,
The verdict is in, it is made by a man.

This is the way it has to be because they think you are just a stupid
old tree!
Now that they are taking you away from me I changed my mind
don't tell me my destiny.
I will find out in due time.
I want to feel the beautiful sun shine.
I'll see you again my friend this I know is not the end.

PLEASE DIM THE LIGHTS

I wish I may, I wish I might,
Be a Valentine Sweetheart for just one night.

If this is not meant to be then the princess crown is just for me.
And yet, no matter what we get,
As long as we are all together everything will be fine,
This fabulous night will be yours and mine.

Close your eyes and you will see,
The beautiful dancing lights are turned to dim from bright for only
    you and me.
You will hear the soft melody,
That carry's your every step into an eternal land of cherished
    memories.

I wish I may, I wish I might,
Find a way to relive this one special night.

I WANNA RIDE BULL

Friends come in all shapes and forms,
This really does not matter so we've been shown.

You can give a small boy a toy but it will not share his love and joy.
He needs someone to talk to and help him when he feels blue.

Someone or thing that belongs to only him,
For only he this friend will bend.
He'll fill the lonely gap within,
This little boys' one and only friend.

We'll always be together and we will take care of each other forever.

Then one day they went to play not knowing that this will be their
    last day.
Why did this happen to you and me?
The cat I did not see!

I knew I let you down as your feathers hit the ground.
A friend like you can never again be found.

What will I do?
I'm so glad that you are the one I found,
To heaven I know is where you are bound.

TAINTED WATERS

Tainted Waters have stolen more than your daughters,
It turned lives to dust and created a world without trust.

It would only have taken a test,
History tells us the rest.
A few drops of chemicals in a machine and the water is clean.

It is too late for some,
That deed has already been done.
Make sure it doesn't happen again,
Watch out for tainted waters my friend.

I'M NOT A LOSER

Everyone wants me to stay in school and most of all follow their rules.
I want to stay home and play, they keep telling me to go away.
You act as though you are the only tool,
Well I'd rather be cool then to put up with your rules.
The day will come when you realize I'm not that dumb,
I know this is thought by some.

It's also been said there will never be a diploma hanging above my
    head,
Most of the negative thoughts you try to put in my head will only
    make me show you how smart I am instead.

I'll walk down the aisle in style while flaunting my PHD,
I'll look you in the face and say "see,"
I'm not disgraced; I did it at my own pace.

Back off and let me go,
Doing it your way I'll never grow.
I may do things a different way and to you it looks like play.

I'm not responsible for your egotistical attitude or your nasty mood.
You aren't going to cause me to brood.
I will complete school this is more important than following your rules.

I will take my Doctrines Degree and I will teach others just like me.
We will have no set pace and they definitely won't feel disgraced.
We will turn learning into fun from me they won't run.
I have to remember what you did to me so I don't send them on a
    foolish spree.

I'm not cruel and I won't use your rules.
I learn just the same, I just quit playing your game.
I work in a very special way,
It really helps the viewer want to stay.
I like the person that I am,
I do the best that I can.

A loser doesn't take a stand or take charge of his life or plan.
I did it the best way I knew how and I didn't throw in the towel.
I'm proud to say teacher's like you are now so few,
Loser I'm not, I took my best shot.
I won and I might add it was fun.

TO EACH HIS OWN

Get out my needles and learn to knit there's a lot you can do besides
    just sit.
If you don't want to do that learn to crochet a stocking cap.
You can always learn how to bake, someday, you'll want to do this for
    your mate.
Then again, first I'd better show you how to cook, in that cupboard is
    the cookbook.

Okay how about learning how to clean,
This should be part of your every day living so it would seem.
Let's embroidery some pillow cases we'll decorate the edges with
    pretty lace.
You can put these things in your hope chest; to make things with
    your own hands is the best.
Oh that's right I forgot things aren't the same,
Girls don't do what we use to do, for this, I don't know who is to
    blame,
I know I wouldn't take this skill away from you.

You're right you should just sit,
You have too many things already to do,
After all we older ladies only had a few.
It's better for you to just complain,
This must be your hobby you now maintain.

I wouldn't want to change the way you are,
Today's women have come so far.
If you don't mind I'll continue to knit,
I'll let you just sit or spend time on trips.

You see I feel we older ones are really the women who have won,
The things you call hard work, for us is fun.
I like to have men open the door and do all the really heavy chores.

It makes me feel good to watch them eat the food I make,
I will never believe all they do is take.
A woman is just as mean as a man, so don't cop out and say your just
    taking a stand.

You be the way you want to be just don't ruin things for the rest of
    the women like me.
I may be from the old school but I guarantee you I'm not the one
    that's the fool.

LIFE

Boy it happens so extremely fast,
That breath you just took is your last.
This is exactly the way it is,
You don't know how long you have to live.

You have no chance to say, hey wait, because you see it's too late.
You don't seem to understand there's no one to lend you a hand.
I'd just finished feeding the kids and picking up the roll a way bed,
All of a sudden there was a pain, I knew no one would be saying my
     name.

I could not breathe and I was cold enough to freeze,
I couldn't comprehend what was said so I knew soon that I would be
     dead.
It happens so very fast; you just don't know if the very next breath is
     your last.

Do you really need to work that extra hour?
It isn't going to earn you more flowers.
I'm begging you to listen to me,
I know what I'm saying so please!

There is no second chance your life is snuffed out in a glance.
No way can you say good-by or ask someone why.
You can't give someone a kiss or say they are the ones you'll miss.
You can't write down your last wishes and it doesn't matter who will
     get your riches.

God was good I have one more time,
What am I doing, I'm living the same old grind.
I guess I'm trying to hide,
I don't want to believe I almost died.

When it's time again no longer can I pretend.
I don't want this to be my last, I can't and don't want to believe life
  goes by so fast.

A TRIBUTE TO MY FATHER

There's no one like my father, he's my knight and shining armor.
He's as wise as the most brilliant scholar.
He's there to conquer all no matter how big or small my problems are.
He's as handsome as Snow White's Prince,
And he's the only man I trust for guidance.
There's no one like my father.

I can still hear him say, "it won't be long before you will no longer
    want to play,
I'll have a terrible time keeping the boys from taking you away."
"Oh daddy I will never leave you," I laugh.
"Yes you will my child but right now your still mine for awhile.
I'm going to enjoy our time together while it lasts."

He always buys me little things, color books, dolls, and Cracker Jack
    rings.
There may be times that he seems stern,
You don't get anything that you don't earn.

Years have gone by, little do I know that it was not only the days that
    were growing nigh?
It seems like yesterday that I was a child and now my dad's walking
    me down the aisle.
I detect a little tear and all of a sudden I feel fear.
He takes me by the hand, "You must understand that this goes along
    with God's plan."
He continues to whispers in my ear, "You'll always be my little girl do
    you hear?
It gives me pride to give this young man my daughter to be his bride."
He looks at me with a smile, "remember you were only mine for a
    little while."

Many things have happened since, heartbreaks and sorrows are now
past tense.
"Oh daddy I wish we could go back and start all over again, I know
let's pretend."
"No sis, you can't go back that way. I thank God and I cherished each
and every day."

My daddy grew ill and I was told it is God's will,
I tried to hide my tears as I watched him for seven years.
He never did complain when he was in so much pain but I knew it
was hard for him to sustain.
I still wanted him to stay even though he was just dwindling away.

I fed him his last meal, it was then God and I made a deal.
"God my daddy's been the best so please let him rest.
I've held on to him so tight so please help me say good-by tonight."

I sit by my daddy's side and hold him tight, "Daddy are you alright?"
I love you more than I can say, Please don't leave me tonight, don't go
away.
"God I changed my mind it just can't be time."
"Listen to me daddy because I know you can hear.
I'll always be your little girl no matter if you're far or near.
I'll always see your smiling face as I grow in grace.
I know in my heart that I'll come home to join you, I am your
daughter and there's no one like you, my father."

DEATH HAS NO FEELING FOR YOU OR ME

I am told my father will soon be gone, ending his life is so wrong.
He gives his children a feeling of security,
Why God are you taking him away from me?

My father is dying at first I feel numb.
All I can do is ask God how come?
When my grandfather died it was the same,
I already knew this deadly game.

I want to reach out and grab his soul,
I want to take it away from death's terrible hold.
I realize the only thing to do is reach over and hold his hand,
Damn!

How much sorrow can I withstand?
I drop to my knee and begin to plea,
"Dear God you can't do this to me!"

I look at my mother, her agony appears,
Oh how old she grows before her years.
I look down at my hands and my fingers are gripped,
This hell and torment goes along with the trip.

The nightmares never cease and I have to pretend to always be at
    peace.
The knot in my gut gets bigger and bigger as I look at him and the
    lump in my throat becomes a trigger.

I cry a million tears and I look like I've aged a million years,
My father's life has disappeared, there's so much I wanted to say but
    instead I chose a game to play.

I wish I was small, I'd hide or climb my tree then I couldn't see or feel
 the pain and agony, maybe I'll just simply fall.
I thought I was prepared; he lingers on,
Friend you're totally wrong if you think you'll ever be ready to say so
 long.

I try to remember what my father said,
"This is one walk you take alone, tears I don't want you to shed as I
 go home."

Old Mr. Death reappears in my life,
He brings an abundance of pain and strife.
Death is the part of reality that will be hard for me to accept with
 dignity.

First my pappy, then my daddy.
You don't have to be old for one thing to see,
Death has no feeling for you or me!

MAMMA

Mamma don't you do like dad,
Don't you die and leave us sad.
I don't want to go through this again,
You won't if you're truly a friend.

I don't think this is fair,
I know everyone cares.
There has to be something that you can do,
Favors you ask are so very few.

Are you afraid of grandma dying?
I know she keeps saying that she is trying.
What are we really put here for?
For him to just watch and adore.
I want more!

I don't want us to have to die,
I don't want to see the family's left behind cry!
What are we going to do?
I guess sit back and bid each other ado.

I'm going to get down on my knees,
I'm going to beg and plead.
Maybe it won't help,
But at least I did something I felt!

Mamma don't you die like dad,
I'm afraid and I feel sad.

YOUR PRESENCE

Listen my friends this has got to come to an end,
I know that you are there,
And I know that you really care.

But when I feel your presence,
Sadness fills my heart in abundance.
It was so hard to lose you,
I know you always knew.

I need to go on with my life,
I have a job to do as a mother and a wife.
Feeling you here fills me with fear.

I know you will never hurt me,
Don't you see?
It's the scent of death I'm running from,
Please let this be done.

I know from heaven you've been sent,
With the angels you went.
I need some peace of mind,
Yes my loving friends it is time.

I want to know that you're at rest,
I want this burden off my chest.
Go to sleep and remember me,
You are comforted through loving Christianity.

My wounds will need to be nurtured,
As I'm living for the future.
This has come to an end,
All my love to you I send.

POVERTY

You know if we'd all stop and think about how lucky we really are,
Just to be able to get up in the morning and walk to our bathrooms
    and take a shower.
To be able to hold our loved ones in our arms and to just live every-
    day life from daylight to dawn.

Now I'm not one to look at things from a negative side,
I guess that has to do with what I call pride.
I know there's times all of us think,
Why don't people take care of their own which kind of stinks?
I've been shown that we all belong to each other,
And I know that every one out there is my brother.

If we don't take a stand and take the weak ones by the hand,
Then what kind of a world is this place, our land?

As Americans we've stood together through wars and depressions,
I don't mind telling you that to me this affliction caused by poverty
    has made one big impression.
It's effecting a big percentage of our generation and the ones to come,
We've got to do something now before we're all done!
There's been no army strong or big enough to tear us apart,
But yet as a person, I know that we've allowed this to get a real good
    start.

I'm going to rest assure that it won't be long before we'll hear,
We've won!
Then I can look at my son with the confidence of a woman that he
    won't have to live in fear for his children,
As we have for all our millions.

We've won another battle,
As we did before!
And we'll continue to do more and more and more!

45

THE CRY'S OF OUR CHILDREN

Listen, Listen, do you hear?
The cry's from our children,
Far and near.

Mommy, daddy, can't you see just what this kind of life is doing to me?

But mommy, daddy, God loaned me to you,
Please don't close your eyes to what's happening and bid me ado.

Oh my sweetheart we're trying to get help for you,
But it takes lots of money to do what we have to do!

But mommy, daddy, I'm afraid,
I don't want to die so young in age.

Hang on my little ones and you will see,
Surely the love and goodness of all the people won't let gangs and
    poverty take you away from me!

Hurry mommy, daddy for I feel faint,
I can see a vision of a saint.
Please don't take me away from my mommy and daddy,
I know they are trying to help me this I believe.
They are getting closer all the time,
I'm going to be just fine.

I know this in my heart,
Even though as I lay here the shadows are growing dark.

Hear my cry's as I rest in peace!
There are more of us children out here who wants to speak.
"Mommy, daddy, hear our cry!
Please don't give up just because we had to say good-by."

Oh my baby's can you hear?
Your mommy and daddy's still out here!
God give us the strength to carry their wish through,
So no more mommy and daddy's have to deal with what we just went
    through!

DISPLACED HOMEMAKER

Don't label me,
Displaced homemaker I don't want to be.
What about the displaced man whom has to be given a hand?

When these words are said it takes us to our knee,
And so many tears we shed,
So Please!

Look at her, no one wants her.
She's one of those, I've been told, a displaced homemaker.

We have been stripped of our titles we held,
And some of them lived lives of pure hell!
We have done no wrong,
We may look weak but we are strong!

You give us hope and you give us dreams,
You tell us we need more self-esteem.
When all the time it's just like before we finally turn the knob to open
     that door,
No, no you don't get anymore!

Can't you see what you are doing to us?
You expect to gain our trust?
We are use to these kinds of names,
The only differences are the players, their names.

You are the weak and we are the strong.
If not, we wouldn't have survived this long.

We have learned more than you,
We can only listen to only a few.
We know in our hearts that we really tried.
And no matter what we still have our pride.

We are women young and old, this I know you've been told.
We will not give up without a fight, this is our one and only plight!

Label us if you will because we are very proud of being the best,
And will be until we draw our last breath.

We want to be free,
Live our own life,
May not be as a wife,
But without the shame that comes with that name!
Don't ever label me!

We are of an old birth,
We are the liberation!
Now let us get on with our education!
Don't give us a taste and then take it away.
All that waste evidently the federal funds have sure gone astray.

Again, don't label me because a displaced homemaker I don't want to
    be!

GRANDDAUGHTER

We call her Billiedelight,
Oh what a big name for such a little tyke.
Her long dark hair flows into locks of curls,
She has a mouth full of beautiful little white pearls.

Great grandma's to blame for her oriental eyes,
A three year old that looks like she is five.

She fights like a wild cat that granddaughter of mine,
Her older brother has quite a time.
She's always knocking him down,
He spends a lot of time on the ground.

The words that flow from that little girl,
Will send most heads a whirl.
She's definitely a tomboy,
Buy her a gun or truck for a toy.

A look from those big blue eyes,
Reassuring you that she can never tell a lie.
Right behind her dad she follows,
She is daddy's little shadow.

What did we do without this child?
Life was much too mild.
She's our dream come true,
Granddaughter, grandma loves you.

GRANDSON

Grandson, grandma was waiting for you,
Yes my little boy you were my dream come true.
It was quite a miracle when your daddy was born,
Just think an added gift to be adorn.

You have the prettiest dark hair,
And you cuddle just like a big old bear.
I see eyes of blue and a dimple or two.

I was there to hear your first cry,
I was so excited I thought I was going to die.
Anyone who denies this feeling would be telling you a lie.

Your mommy and daddy had you all picked out,
You are the one,
Your dad's number one son.
There's no doubt.

Don't grow up to fast my dear,
Not having enough time to spend with you is my fear.
Grandson you're my pride and joy,
I couldn't have asked for a better boy.

Always remember one thing,
When you put on your girl's finger that ring,
Your old grandma's still around,
I hope there will be time for me that you've found.
I pray memories of me will bring you joy,
Just as you do for me my beautiful grandbaby boy.

SON

Son you are very important to me,
Through the years we've accumulated a lot of memories.
I know there were times it seemed to you,
You would just as soon bid me ado.
You now surely know that these feelings were never true.

I love and cherish you from the bottom of my heart,
I only wanted the best for you from the start.
You are exactly what I prayed for,
You are my one and only son whom I adore.

I told you it wouldn't be long,
Before you'd grow up to be strong.
You are my dream come true,
Thank God I have a son like you.

We've had some pretty rough times it seems,
But I think we've made a pretty good team.
I know it was tough growing up without a dad,
And I know there were a lot of times you felt sad.
I heard you, son, all the time,
This is when a man entered our lives yours and mine.

I look at you now and you are a man.
All I can say is wow, I will always be your number one fan.
Now you have little ones to look up to you,
They will be proud to say they come from you.
It will be hard at times you will see,
When this happens look back and think this is why they did the
    things they did to me.

Keep this tucked in your heart,
They loved me dearly right from the start.

They will fight for me until the end,
They're not just my parents they're also my friends.

Sometimes you take my breath away,
When I watch you with your kids play.
You deal with them so tenderly,
Thank you God for giving my son to me.

I hope we gave you some good memories,
As we grow old don't forget to think of me,
Son I'm very proud to say,
I know you'll never be far away.

I strut down the street with my head held high,
Do you know why?
This man is my son I cry!

When I leave this earth I will know,
You have filled me with pride as I go.
I will hold my head high and I know you will cry,
But wipe away the tears, we had some wonderful years.
There's only one reason for me to have been here,
Watching you has made this very clear.

You are a gentle soul with love so deep,
It takes a true man like you who is not afraid to weep.
For you I will place a special star in the sky,
Look at it son when you begin to cry.
It's me on the other side looking at you with a mother's pride.

It will be your turn to carry on,
For your children and grandchildren I know you will be strong.
This is who you are and I will always love you even from afar.
My one and only son, I will smile when this day is done.

IT'S NOT THE END

Someone has taken this mother's place,
The time is truly here.
I see it in your face,
I'm really filled with fear.

What is going to happen to me now that this period of my life is
   through?
I don't want to go back in a corner like an old shoe.

Let me tell you where I'm coming from,
The job I started has just begun.
We've shared many tears all through these years.
We've shared many joys and tender smiles for each other,
I've found that I've tried to be a good mother.

We have had our share of fights,
A little pat or smile by sight.
We knew we were saying to each other,
Hey that's all right.

I know what I've lost through my later years,
Changed my high peaks of joy to tears.
The closeness and love from the friends that I've had,
To think I forgot makes me mad.

I no longer feel I have to hide,
You help reinforce my positive side.
I'm sharing with you the feelings that I have inside,
You've given me the strength to fulfill the goals that I thought had
   died.

If only you knew,
I found this in you.
I am very proud to have a son like you.

Let's not disburse and go our own way,
And lose contact with each other through the upcoming days.
Let's continue to stand together as a family and have some fun,
And finish the job we've begun.

Hey look at us we did it,
At times it was rough, admit it!
You know the old saying,
"You've come a long way baby,"
Well maybe but we've got a long way to go this we all know.

Let's hold each other's hand,
You know we still need someone to understand.
No matter when I'll always be your friend.
Thank you for being who you are,
You are my number one star!

Someone has taken this mother's place,
I will bough out as best I can.
I hope you understand,
I want to do this with grace.

This is not the end,
I'm not only your mother I'll always be your friend.

DAUGHTER-IN-LAW

To this day you still say, "why don't you love me to?"
If only you knew but maybe in time you will realize that you are truly
    a daughter of mine.
You will see how much you mean to me, and we will then be just fine.

You were only fifteen when you came into my heart,
You thought I was so mean right from the start.
I tried to chase you away by telling you not to stay.
I knew that was not in the plan as you and my son took a stand.

The two of you were young in years,
Even so, young or old, the love you felt for each other was pretty
    clear.
As I watched the two of you I knew, no girl will matter to my son but
    you.

I began to get excited, I'm finally going to have a daughter and I'm
    really delighted.
I want to teach you all that I know which are a lot of skills that came
    from my mom and grandma to you I will show.

I want to welcome you into my home and assure you that you will
    never again be alone.
I want you to know that you can count on me,
Easy for the two of you I want it to be.

You are the one that fills my son's life with joy,
You honor him by giving him a boy.
Later a daughter joins you as his number one,
I look at the four of you at the end of the day, I must say, I know this
    is good what has been done.

I am really proud to say as I get down on my knees and pray,
Thank you God for opening our door and allowing such a wonderful
    girl to come in and explore.

I am so very proud that you are here,
I will always keep you in my heart and near.
You are my girl I've seen in my dreams,
I know that through the years we have made a pretty good team.

I want you to take this with you forever that I could not have asked
    for anyone better.
You are a wonderful wife and mother, and yes, you are a wonderful
    daughter.
Please stop wondering why I don't love you to, because daughter of
    mine, I do.

MY HUSBAND

Darling of mine we've had quite a time,
I look at you and I can't help but sigh.
I won't tell a lie, our hair is now turning gray and I still say,
You still take my breath away.

You are a very handsome man,
And just as loving as before.
Without you I can not stand,
You are the one I will always adore.

You were a gift to my son and I,
You came into our lives when I was ready to die.
You gave us hope and showed us how to cope,
You held us in your arms and kept us from harm.

I think my son and I also gave you a reason to be,
So you see,
This was the true plan, you were meant to be my man.
We had some rocky times but I knew that we would be fine.
We were meant to be, we three.

Our son and daughter-in-laws' family is almost grown,
Let this be known, we are so proud of the two of you,
You are an amazing couple one of a few.
We will always love you, just for you.

Darling our years together went by really fast,
This love for you will always last.
If I pass before you my dear, never fear,
I will be near.

So take this old lady with gray hair,
And let's pass through the rest of this life as though we are at the fair.
I want to laugh and hold you close to me,
This is truly the way it should be.
Darling of mine we've had quite a time,
Don't forget to please look for me then you will see, again, everything
    will be fine.

CHARLES

You are not my birth father but you have done more for me than any
   other.
For a man who isn't physically tall, you sure did it all.
My mom was left alone so young, thinking she will never again have
   fun.
There you were all the time, delivering furniture, but we were still
   blind.
Little did you and my mother know that someday with each other
   you would grow old.

My biological father left me when I was thirty-four,
I truly believed no other man could open that door.
There you were with a smile on your face ready to take your place.
When I first seen you I was so aware, all I could do was stop and
   stare,
You looked so much like my birth father you see,
But that isn't what allowed you to take your place with me.

You were a gentle loving man that had also lost someone so I
   understand.
With your wife and my father appearing so near, I believe they sent
   you to us to take away our fear.
You needed us when all was said and done, life will be better because
   we have all won.

Whatever the reason I'm so glad we have you,
A person like you are so far and few.
Thank you dad for joining our clan, through this life we will go hand
   in hand.
We will be blessed for evermore because you walked through our
   door.

IS IT TIME ?

It's surely not time; this is our lives, yours and mine.
Why?
Why does it all have to end?
I don't want to give it up my friend.
The memories will always last because a giant shadow you all did cast!

I can still hear the laughter and I can feel the sorrow.
Even tomorrow different aromas will fill the air, as I see the visions of
    all that care.
I want to share this wonderful childhood and I hope that you have
    understood.
This kind of a bond will never be gone.

Now it's time to bid all of you ado,
Set aside the old and bring in the new.
Why?
We can use the mixture of the two I cry!
Remember the old will help the new just try!

It's time,
This is our lives, yours and mine.
Now I believe we will be fine so thank you for making what was
    yours, mine.

FOR MY BROTHERS

You know it was really hard on me,
I was the only girl and in the middle of us three.
Sometimes I didn't know whether to fight or cry,
Sometimes I'd just sit and ask myself why?
Why was I the only young female around,
This was a creation for trouble I found.

Even though we fought with each other,
There had better be no one who hurt my brothers.
You spent most of your young lives trying to make me tame, what a
    shame.
The fun and games, you know things just would not have been the
    same.

Each one of you is very special to me, without you where would I
    now be?
I miss all the times that we had, I miss all the good and the bad.
I'm glad I was able to take this journey with you, I will always be
    there for you but this you knew.

I will think of our plight as I lay at night and a smile will appear,
I feel so warm and blessed to know that we will always be near.

AS TIME GOES BY

Who is this wrinkled faced lady I see,
Surely that cannot be me.
I don't feel any different than I did when I was a kid.
As I continue to look in the mirror I hear, heaven forbid.

Look at the lid's sag over my eyes,
You can't see that they are as blue as the sky.
The crater wrinkles around my mouth are so deep,
My goodness, this must happen while I'm asleep.
There are brown spots all over my hands and face,
It's really hard for me to realize what has taken place.

Working hard is no problem for me, not one bit,
I am now a lot more physically fit.
I'm more emotionally and mentally stable than ever before,
But still I will never be the same for evermore.

It's so clear what happens to you and me,
It's our soul inside that's still young and free,
That's why even though our reflection has changed, we feel the same.

What a terrible reality for me, our bodies and mind grows old and dies,
While our soul is still young and doing fine.
It's your body and mind that goes away,
Your soul still wants to play.
Let's hope it's able to go on and live, it still has so much to give.

My body, mind, and soul needs to age the same,
So that as I look in the mirror there will be no game.
I will then know and expect an ugly old lady to be there,
In this mirror I cannot help but still stare.
I smile now as I remember what my grandma did say,
Who's this ugly old lady that's starring back at me today?

FOR THOSE WHO HAVE TOUCHED MY LIFE

For all those who have touched my life through the years,
Remember me as the one who really cared.
Each and every one of you was a link in the chain that sent me
    through.
Without one of these links I'm afraid to think of the drastic change
    that would have been made or how it would have been played.
Thank goodness it went just as it was planned because I think my life
    has been really grand.

I am thankful to have shared with you even a day because it made
    such a difference I must say.
Whether it was good or we think it was bad, we had an experience
    that otherwise we wouldn't have had.
Hopefully the lesson did not go unheard because to close your mind
    is totally absurd.

It's hard to understand the plan,
We must walk away from all of this with the knowledge that we've
    been blessed when taking someone by his or her hand.
This is a journey in itself, I couldn't have done this without your help.
For all of those who have touched my life through the years, There
    will be no tears and I will walk into another time without any
    fears.